Lyrical Literature
A WHISTLE-STOP TOUR OF THE CLASSICS!

EDWIN CHARLES

To my grandmother on her 101st birthday
08.11.2023

Contents

READER, I MARRIED HIM

Jane Eyre

Let me start and speak and share
About a young girl called Jane Eyre.
She grew up thinking she was bad
For such a wicked aunt she had,
Who told her she was filthy rude
And took away her toys and food
Then smacked her with a witch's broom
And locked her in a haunted room.
And when the aunt had had enough
She treated her extremely rough,
And sent her off to Lowood school
Where she was taught by rod and rule.

There Mr Brocklehurst did make
Her stand up on her stool and spake
Her lessons loud in French and Greek
And then forbade the girl to speak!
She stood upon that stool for weeks
As sombre tears ran down her cheeks.

Then little Helen Burns did give
Her bread she stole to let her live,
And then she scribed upon her slate
From Rasselas to change her fate,
But little Helen laughed then cried
And in the morning she had died!

Poor Jane was left there all alone
As other girls chilled to the bone,
Most of the girls did sadly die
But not our Jane, oh she did try
To live and learn and she did this
But surely life it had more bliss?
If only happiness could reach her
Perhaps she would become a teacher?

So this she did, and years did pass
Until one day it came at last,
A notice in the post no less
An advert for a governess!

So off she went away from all
And ended up at Thornfield Hall

Where she was welcomed gay and sprightly
By Mrs Fairfax in her nightie
Who said, 'My dear you've come a way
Your bedchamber's along this way,'
And down a spooky corridor
With candles and a flagstone floor
Did Jane reside and cry at night
But haunting sounds gave her a fright -
She thought the noise was one Grace Poole
But Fairfax said she was a fool,
She thought she must be going mad
Presumed it was the wine she'd had!

She had to teach a girl Adele
To speak in French and dress as well,
But days were long and very steady
Till one day she bewitched a neddy
Whose rider, tall and dark, and strange
Fell off and said to her with rage
'You witch you have upset my horse,
I'm Mr Rochester of course!'

She said, 'Oh dear, are you all right?
I must have given you a fright,
Your horse reared up from out the fog
But what a gorgeous shaggy dog
You have with you, oh what's his name?
Oh please don't shame me with the blame!'

He groaned a deep disgruntled sound
And scrambled back up off the ground,
'His name is Pilot, wicked hound
And now I'm leaving, homeward bound
To Thornfield Hall, where I am master!'
Jane thought, *Oh what a huge disaster,*
I've now so nearly killed my master,
And left him with his leg in plaster!

When she got back she found him crude,
Impertinent and really rude,
But when she talked to him at length
She found within her wit and strength;
She'd met her match and he'd met his
So this was love - what perfect bliss!

But Jane was just a simple lass
And he was vulgar, rich, and crass,
He used a girl, they called her Blanche,
To make Jane cry, her love enhance;
His action it was overzealous,
But boy did it make Jane so jealous!

She ran back to her aunt and cried
'My heart it bleeds, I've nearly died!'
'But now,' said aunt, 'you've got some cash
I hid it in a healthy stash,
And now I'm on my death bed I
Will give you it before I die!'

4

So Jane went back and said, 'Okay
If you behave then I will stay,'
And Rochester swore on his life
And asked our Jane to be his wife!

Up to the altar she was carried
But then found out that he was married -
And there she was all shocked and static
With ex-wife locked up in the attic!

The mad old wife was still alive
And Jane ran off and cried and cried,
She nearly died upon the moor
But some nice chap did her adore,
He scooped her up and made her see
That she'd survive the misery!

But Jane did long for Thornfield Hall
And in a dream, she heard him call -
She bolted fast back down the hill
But all was deathly quiet, still,
And there in woods without a sound
Was Thornfield Hall, burnt to the ground!

The mad old wife had burnt it down
Broke from her nurse and tore her gown,
She'd jumped from top of burning Hall
And killed herself as she did fall!

Poor Rochester gave Jane a fright
He'd gone quite blind and lost his sight,
But Jane did love him through and through
And love for him just grew and grew!

The end turned out not quite so grim
For reader, she did marry him!

Pride and Prejudice

This famous fiction work of old
Starts when a great big house is sold,
Its owner is a wealthy squire
To whom five daughters do aspire
For each of them does want to be
Rich, and loved, and fine and free.

The eldest two are Jane and Lizzie
One is fair, the other's frizzy,
Their mother is the most obsessed
And sends their pa at her behest
To meet this man, which he does grimly
And finds out that his name is Bingley.

The girls all jump around with joy
But how to meet this dashing boy?
'I know,' said Ma one rainy day,

'Go over there, you'll have to stay!'
She sent the eldest one on Nelly
(A big old brute but rather smelly),
And when a vicious storm rained down
The girl arrived with soaking gown!

And Mr Bingley's sisters were
Appalled and quite ashamed of her,
How could a girl whose aim was marriage
Arrive at theirs without a carriage?!
They took her to a stately room
And sent the horse off with the groom.
The servants warmed and gave her food
The sisters supercilious and rude.

But Mr Bingley was impressed
And while she stayed became obsessed,
But his best mate, a chap called Darcy
Began to get quite cross and arsey,
He told him she was brash and coarse
And sent her home upon her horse!

But eldest girl was hurt and lost
She must have him at any cost,
So mother pulled out all the stops
And took her to expensive shops.
But all the girls around the place
Were also set upon this chase
To get the rich and wealthy man
By hook or crook or lying plan!

But no one had as much persistence
As Mrs Bennet's strong resistance;
She took the girls with sheer delight
In finest gowns on darkest night
And all five girls out-did them all
At Mr Bingley's winter ball!

But at this ball they all drank wine
And had a fine and dandy time,
But they forgot to always be
Genteel, polite, and womanly.

Fitzwilliam Darcy was ashamed
The ghastly mother was to blame,
So he refused to dance with Lizzie
Which sent the mother in a tizzy,
And she pronounced and said aloud
That he was sanctimonious and proud!

The sisters jeered and said with snide
'That boy is vanity and pride!'
This made our Darcy curse and frown,
So he went off to London Town
And took with him the Bingley lot
And Bennet girls he quite forgot!

Then one fine day at Longbourn Manor
A weird old man with lisp and stammer
Turned up, and announced on his life
That he'd take Lizzie for his wife -

He pleaded gushing deeply longings
But no way she'd take Mr Collins!
For he was ugly, poor, a vicar,
Which only made her mother bicker
For she wanted her 'Yes' to say
So Longbourn wasn't entailed away!

But then the twists and turns began
And entered quite a dashing man -
But dark and devilish, the toad
Set out to get the money owed.
His mind it would not rest or still
Since he felt diddled from a will
From Mr Darcy's dear old dad
Who recognised he was a cad.
So lies did Wickham spill to all
At card party and Brighton Ball,
Whence he took off with youngest lass
In spite, revenge, and after cash!

But then the truth began to chill
For lies to girls did Wickham spill:
Before he'd wooed the Bennet child,
Whose temperament was rather wild,
He'd not just charmed, and spooned, and kissed her
But he'd abducted Darcy's sister!

Meanwhile, Darcy saw something
In Lizzie's eyes which made him sing,
And when they danced at Rosings Park
He wrote a letter in the dark
Telling her the bitter truth -
Which put our Lizzie through the roof!

But passion was alighted when
She read said letter, wept, and then
When she'd digested words enclosed
He got down on one knee, proposed!

She said, 'But you betrayed my sister,
Not Wickham one, that one who kissed her,
But golden Jane who loves with heart
That gorgeous boy from Netherfield Park!'

Mr Darcy coughs and stammers
She said, 'Your ungentlemanlike manners
Have cost you here, I don't accept!'
So she refused Darcy's request
Who promptly jumped into a lake
And came out looking like a rake!

Meanwhile, the father went to find
His girl before she came a bride -
He raced off with no hesitation
To save his girls their reputation,
He summoned lots of carriages
To save his daughters' marriages,

And found the silly girl unmarried
So to the altar she was carried,
She wed the cad and went to Yorkshire
And that was how he saved his daughter!

But little did the others know
That Darcy had his love bestowed;
By bribing Wickham with his stash
Who took the girl and kept the cash!

When Lizzie learnt the sister wedded
She found to whom she was indebted,
For Darcy it was not mistaken
Had triumphed here and saved her bacon!

His pride to him did not belong
When he admitted he was wrong
To stop belovèd Jane from loving
With prejudice concealed and gloving!

So Jane and Bingley duly wed
And as the vows were being said
Our Mr Darcy asked once more
If it was him she did adore,
And now that she did understand
Would Lizzie now give him her hand?

And this she did, and wedded bliss
Was sealed there with a loving kiss!
And do you know the moral here,
Which all our hearts and souls hold dear
Is that a single rich man's life
Is not complete without a wife -
For it's a universal truth
And Liz and Darcy are the proof!

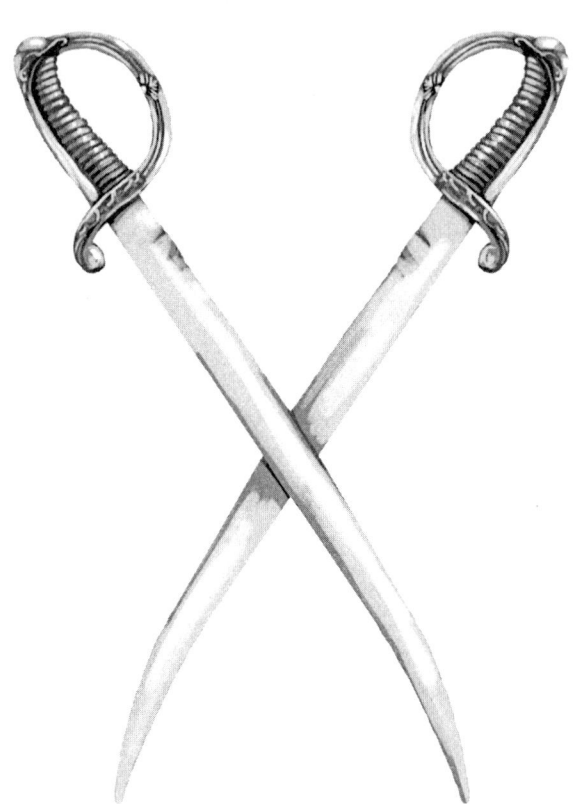

War and Peace

This one taxed me when I read
So listen or you'll lose the thread,
And I will try to here condense
Six hundred thousand words to sense!

The tale starts in St Petersburg
With opulence and girls in furs
And fine young men in gold regalia
And medals, swords, and paraphernalia.

You see Napoleon has burst forth
And he's invading Europe's north
So Russia's sabres are all drawn
But still they dance and drink till dawn!

So Anna Pavlovna has this gaff
Where champagne flows from large carafes,
We meet five social families
Who all have great calamities!

I'll start with Pierre cos he's the lead
He is a count, a Bezukhov indeed.
But he is illegit as such
So no one really cares that much
About that plainest of young men,
Until his uncle dies, and then
He's suddenly extremely rich,
And all the girls they start to bitch
Over Pierre, once in the gutter
But now he's rich their fans do flutter!

So that's Pierre, but his best friend
Andrei Bolkonsky's ear does bend,
For Andrei's married, but cares not
For pretty wife and unborn tot
That she is carrying to term
But not yet had – of that we'll learn!

Okay, that's them, but there's his sister
Princess Bolkonsky, she's a spinster,
She's religious, plain, and weepy,
She's dressed in black and rather creepy!

Then there's this brother sister duo
Who social climb and drink, you know,

Like some of those you see today
You see them from a mile away!
Anyway, that girl Hélène,
Well, she's a favourite with the men -
She absolutely ravishing
And gets Bezukhov lavishing
His wealth on her, allures the fool
And soon she's married him, and cruel
She is for days and weeks and years
And this reduces him to tears!

So back to Andrei and his wife
Cos she's now fighting for her life,
Cos while she's pushing, giving birth
She starts to scream and swear and curse,
And poor young girl, she sadly dies,
And Andrei, well, he cries and cries -
Cos he then sees she meant so much,
But now she's dead and he's got such
A cross to bear, regret and shame
And spends weeks cursing God with blame!

He loses all his faith and trust
And vows to never fall for lust -
The baby lives so that bit's happy
An heir and spare in cotton nappy
A single dad but that's okay
For lots of wives died in that day!

Back to plot and there's another
Family - a girl and brother,
She is fine and beautiful
And he is brave and dutiful.
He's obsessed with going to war
And she wants a hubby, a house, and more.
She's Natasha, he is Nick,
There's also Sonya - she's a side-kick -
She's their cousin and she is poor
But secretly Nick does her adore;
They are the Rostovs and they come a crasher
When Andrei Bolkonsky falls for Natasha,
Cos at the same time bro Nicky ain't able
To keep himself far from the gambling table!

So Rostovs lot lose all their capital
And though Natasha is pretty and affable,
The old Prince Bolkonsky, Andrei's father
Says he dislikes her, and he would rather
He wed a girl who's more remunerable
So tells Andrei she's not pursuable;
And Andrei's sad for he's quite smitten
Since finally his heart's been bitten
With gushing love, so he does plead
And Prince Bolkonsky does concede -
Condition is he'll wait a year
Nattie says her love's so dear
That she can wait for him, but doubts
And worries war will now break-out,
And waiting such a great long time

When she's all ripe and in her prime
Will make her fret and lose her mind
When he sods off, leaves her behind!

But she comes later, first of all
All the men go off to war,
There's a massive fight, they all nearly die
But somehow they live, with relief they all cry!

Then back in Moscow that wife with posh air -
You know, the one that married Pierre,
Well, she's a naughty one that minx,
And when her hubby turns and blinks
She sleeps with his friend Dolokhov,
Seduced over beef stroganoff!

How could Hélène be so cruel?!
Bezukhov's cross, sets up a duel,
So Mr Pierre and the cheating brute
Aim loaded guns, but which one will shoot?
Which one will shoot first and which one will cry?
Which one will get Hélène, which one will die?

Pierre shoots first and injures the sinner,
So he's won the day and now he's a winner
But he isn't happy cos his anaclysis
Reveals a compounded existential crisis!
So he gets all weird and all philanthropic -
See Tolstoy is deep here and most philosophic!

Back to Natasha, and while Andrei's off
With General Kutuzov and Nicky Rostov,
She falls for that chap who's constantly braggin'
That devilish boy Anatole Kuragin...

So during that year that she's meant to be faithful
She loses her mind, and acts quite disgraceful
When Andrei returns, he's downright appalled
What happened to the girl who he had adored?!

So she's a disgrace with a bad reputation
And everyone's injured by this aberration -
Most keenly of all the Rostovs' mother,
Cos she'd had her hopes on the useless brother;
That Nicky she hoped would marry for money
But he adores Sonya which just isn't funny,
Cos she is his cousin, and this is just incest
But Princess Bolkonsky perks up his interest
Cos he helps to save the life of her brother -
That Andrei boy that's the hope of his mother
That Natasha did lose by the will of her action,
And all of this adds to her gross stupefaction!

But just as Natasha sipped her cappuccino
A battle ensued at this place Borodino,
And Anatole's blown to a thousand pieces -
And here's where the gravitas increases!
For Andrei's also been badly hurt,
And as he's lying there covered in dirt,
That cad Anatole does now apologise

For stealing the love from his virginal bride!

So when Andrei comes back in a right old mess
Natasha comes in in this beautiful dress
And kneels down beside him, stroking his brow,
Remorseful, ashamed for this terrible row
And he's slowly dying and breathing his last
And she's sat there crying, regretting the past
And just at the point when they were reconciled,
He started to moan and annoyingly died!

So she's broken hearted and runs to Pierre,
But he's gone bananas and had this nightmare
That it is his destiny to murder Napoleon,
Believing he's some kind of reborn Timoleon...

But he gets captured and now is a slave
And the French bind him up and take him away.
But then the French army are on the retreat -
They're starving in Moscow with nothing to eat -
So on their way back as they're weak at the knees
The Russians take fire from the woods and the trees,
And Dolokhov, you know, the one that Pierre
Did shoot with a bullet he shot through the air
For shagging his wife and betraying his trust,
Jeopardising friendship and satisfying lust;
Well, he's now a hero and Count Pierre's saviour
And Pierre now forgives his atrocious behaviour,
Especially so when that unfaithful wife
Then poisons herself and takes her own life.

See how Tolstoy brings it together?
My goodness that Russian is mightily clever!

But what of Natasha and Nicky and co?
Well, Sonya releases her love for him so
That he can now marry the Princess to show
That Maria, whose brother was Andrei you know,
That she is the one who is most sacrificial;
For Rostovs this marriage is most beneficial,
For they get their riches and live happily -
And lastly not leastly for that family,
Who suffered the losses, the burdens, the pain,
Well they triumph all now with double the gain -
For Tasha has always adored that Pierre,
He's moral, he's honest, he's faithful, he's fair –

And here is the teaching that Tolstoy is making
Through soul searching, death, and the giving and taking
In heartbreak, forgiving, in grief and release
Is learning and living through war and through peace!

Mansfield Park

This tale is of a loving heart,
There's pain and sorrow from the start;
A poor young girl from Portsmouth went
Away from home and north was sent
To rich and wealthy family
Where mother sent her happily -
The reason was that she did moan
She had too many of her own,
Too many kids and mouths to feed
And Fanny Price she did not need.

So little Fanny took the journey
Reaching Northampton far too early,
The carriage came, then after dark
She finally arrived at Mansfield Park!

The drunken brother Tom was there
And not a jot for her did care,
He sent her to his Auntie Norris
Who lied and broke her faithful promise -
For she had said she'd take her niece
If only just to keep the peace!

But when the girl on doorstep landed
She postulated plain and candid
She said to Thomas Bertram, 'Sir,
I cannot take this silly girl!
You must allow her to reside
With you instead,' she said with snide!

So little Fanny Price was took
And in the attic she was put,
They brought her up but made it plain
That she was paying for her shame,
For she was poor and had no right
And she'd be kept, but out of sight
For her they had no inclination
For she was just their poor relation!

The cousins were a frightful bore
And Fanny Price they did ignore
Except for one, the second son
Who lavished her with joy and fun -
They wrote, and rode, and laughed, and played,
But this just made his dad dismayed,

He said, 'Young Edmund, Fanny is
Your poor relation, listen kid
You must betroth a rich grand lady,'
His motives they were dark and shady!

And when he went off to Antigua
The plan to rid her just got meaner,
Because the aunt had now invited
Some rich young girl who Fanny slighted
Because this Mary girl did like
Her Edmund, so she raged in spite
Because the plan was for her to
Betroth the brother, Fanny knew
That Mary wanted Edmund for
Herself to hold and to adore!

And not just that, for Mary had
A brother, who was quite the cad,
These Crawfords they did charm them all
At Fanny Price's coming-out ball!

Then when proposal from the brother
Came to our Fan, she ran to mother
In Eastbourne, where she cried in pain
And wrote to Edmund for her shame
She said, 'I don't love Henry Crawford
His manners they are false and awkward,
His sole pursuit is being loved
His scope for love is thinly gloved!

He's full of swankest pomp and hype
And frankly he's just not my type!'

But Henry tried and he insisted,
He bought her gifts and he persisted
In wooing her, but she would not
Accept that boy at any cost.
His gifts and cards did not impress
And this left Henry all depressed.

Meanwhile, Miss Mary tried her hand
To get that priceless wedding band -
But when she found that her prospective
Had clergyman for life elected
She changed her mind, and quickly spun
A plan to get the eldest son!
When he came back from West Indies
She fell for him with weakened knees,
But he was drunk and reckless too
And Mary's plan it all fell through!

And then when Henry Crawford took
A liking for a famous book
It was the married sister he
Did set about to flirt and please,
But Edmund's sister had just married -
Across the threshold she'd been carried
By weird old Rushworth proud and stupid,
But still our Henry he played cupid

He wooed and bedded thick Mariah
And she was cast a social pariah!

So Crawfords did retreat and fast
Their colours were revealed at last,
They went back off to London Town
And Bertrams did bemoan and frown,
But little Fanny Price was right
She saw through all their pride and spite,
And finally our Edmund did
See that his love inside was hid,
And though this tale's tempestuous
It's also quite incestuous,
And this provoked a wild discussion
For Edmund was our Fanny's cousin!

But after much deliberation,
Much disgrace and speculation,
The boy and girl did wed at end
And all the fall-out did thus mend!

Like all of Austen's famous tales
With stupid boys and wise females,
We see that Fanny Price was right
To fight for Ed with all her might.

Her love for him was always targeted
To living in that glorious parsonage,
And there they lived in peace and kissed
In perfect harmony and bliss!

The lesson is for stupid men
Who chase and flirt but find that then,
The one they love with all their heart
Was always there right from the start!

Far From the Madding Crowd

Okay, this one is not for fools
So listen up and down your tools,
Like men who worked and women too
With scythes and shears in summers blue;
And one Bathsheba Everdene
Who roamed the lanes and pastures green,
And toiled the land, and worked a farm
Bewitched a shepherd with her charm.

She toyed with him and made him sweat
And left him troubled with regret -
For one fine day he brought a lamb
But in his face the door did slam,
For on that day as she reposed
He flattered her and then proposed!
Of weakness she suspected him
And promptly she rejected him.

And then she got all high and mighty
(She'd always been quite rash and flighty),
Her uncle had her quite preferred
And then bequeathed his farm to her.

So off she went in horse and cart
To resurrect his farm, and start
A business selling tonnes of wheat -
In man's world this was no mean feat,
For in those days a woman's lot
Was cradling babies in the cot.
The woman couldn't do much more
Than cook and clean and scrub the floor,
So when Miss E became the boss
And sold the corn for twice the cost
The farmer men were quite put out,
Who was this girl with rosy pout
Who thought her better than the men
And fired the lazy among them?

But then one day that Shepherd Oak
You know, the meek and useless bloke,
Lost all his flock upon a hill
And couldn't pay his rental bill,
So he turned up at Everdene's
And all the men were thrilled and pleased
For he was a great shepherd bloke,
But missy *still* thought him a joke.

One day with friend and flirts and winks
She bought a card the naughty minx!
A valentine sent as a joke
To some poor unsuspecting bloke
Would make them laugh, their lives enrich,
Relieve the boredom of cross-stitch!

They flipped a book to choose a guy
To send it to, see his reply
The man the joke was sent unto
Was old and grey and loaded too -
His name was Mr Boldwood see
And here began his misery,
For when she put him under spell
Proposal came from him as well!

Now she again did not reply
This made the old man cry and cry,
For he did love her to distraction -
Evidently by his reaction!
For when she chose another chap
With swords, red coat, and sergeant's cap,
He went quite mad and shot him dead
And guillotine was at his head.
This Sergeant Troy had married her
And with his charm had carried her
Along a sinful, wicked path
Of lies, deceit, the aftermath
Of which was misery and tears
And this went on for years and years!

Then one day truth came out and Troy
Transpired a wicked naughty boy
For he had village girl so mild,
Corrupted, and left her with child!

When Fanny Robin died of cold
The truth was finally thus told
Then Sheba screamed, Troy ran away
And left his clothes there in the bay,
It was assumed that he had died
Bathsheba took this in her stride
And then said Boldwood she would marry,
Across the threshold he would carry
But then Troy came and shocked her head
And that's why Boldwood shot him dead!

And then the whole thing goes quite bad
And Sheba cries and goes quite mad,
You see she's learnt of love and pain
And injury and lies and strain.
She sees at end her long for lust
Was stupid for the goal was trust,
And all along the perfect lad
Was in the lambing fields she had!

But right when she saw blatant truth
Our Shepherd Oak went through the roof -
He'd had a gut of her rejection
He saw her pride at close inspection!
So he then left her, she then crying
Since farm was screwed and sheep were dying,
So galloped off she did to plead
For him to save the sheep indeed!

And Hardy hypes our true elation
By reconciling their relation,
You see the point you must take heed
Is where *you are* is what you need
And Sheba wants you girls to see
How my love slighted me, me, me!
So all you girls there in your prime
Let no man steal your thyme, your thyme
Let no man steal your thyme, your thyme,
Let no man steal your thyme!

The Tenant of Wildfell Hall

Now here's a book I really rate -
A woman who controls her fate
By getting out from man's restrictions
Believing in her own convictions!

The story starts all secretive
Upon the moors this lady lives
In solitude, there with her son
In widows weeds her secret's spun;
By being single in a Hall
She hoped that she would fool them all.

But in the village, they did question
The motives for her life's election
For who would choose a gloomy house

Then creep about like silent mouse?
For under veil and false regalias
Was pseudonym and made-up alias!

The folk in town became suspicious
But Gilbert Markham felt auspicious
For stranger he had longing for
Something he hadn't felt before...

So one fine day he does suggest
A sea view for her to ingest
And draw and paint from inspiration -
Which she accepts with hesitation.

The day comes forth, it's clear and mild
The view's bewitching, queer and wild,
And as the sun sets in the cold
The purple moor then turns to gold,
He whispers long into her ear;
'This happens here but twice a year,
I tell you this it is my duty
For no rich man could own such beauty!'

It's then that Helen's heart that slept
Comes back to life for he has depth,
He may be plain and own no mansion
But he is devilishly handsome!

But she must to her secret keep
For though she loves him she does weep;
For to another man she is
Betrothed, so cannot now be his!

She does not think she can disclose
To Gilbert, truth of which she knows,
But risk she takes for she believes
He'll understand her when he reads
Her diary, which she has scribed
About the drunken man who lied
And cheated on her countless times,
Infected marriage with his lies
And ruined mind of her dear son
With drink and killing with his gun.

When Gilbert read the diary
He rushed up to the Hall with speed
But when he got there she had left
Poor Gilbert he was quite bereft,
So in a carriage he did get
To Grassdale Manor off he set!

When he arrived our Helen said,
'My husband's ill but not yet dead!'
'But you must leave the brute!' he cried,
'For he has your whole life denied -
You're starved of love, and care, affection
I want to offer you protection!

Come back with me and leave this place
That husband is a crude disgrace
The ass will die eventually
And then you're free to marry me!'

But Helen had to stick it out -
She stayed with the old drunken lout,
You see back then she'd made a vow
You couldn't just divorce as now -
So stayed she did with ticking bomb
Abound to Mr Huntingdon.

But Huntingdon was very ill
He coughed up blood but even still
He drank, and swore, and spat, and hissed,
And waved at her his dirty fist;
She bore it like a saint she did
And from his face the tears she hid.

Like martyr who keeps going through
The pain and suffering, she knew
That one day Huntingdon would die -
And when he did, oh she did cry
For she had made it her end-goal
To try to save his withered soul!

But that old drunk did not repent
And so to hell the brute was sent!
But Helen did not castigate
Herself for saving reprobate,

For she had tried right from the start
Through virtue in the female heart,
And there right at the very end
Her heart eventually does mend -
For have you guessed? After the hurt
She ended up with hunk Gilbert!

The moral here is heroinism
In bravery and feminism,
And really all you girls should look
To learn something here from this book -
The way to get your just deserves
When bastard men get on your nerves
Is to reside on moral heights
And stand up for your women's rights
So stick with it, don't walk away
And learn from dearest Anne Brontë!

Wives and Daughters

Okay, this one is lesser told
But it's a gem, a work of gold;
It starts there in a great big pile
A little girl with sweetest smile
Whose dad's a widower you see
And she's alone in misery
But he loves her, she's prized, and spruced
Which gets her through the pain induced.

But at the start that's where she finds
Where Lady Hollingford resides
That she is done with grace and glee
And falls asleep under a tree!

When Dad comes back to pet her head
He finds that she's been put to bed
By Hyacinth, this flaunting witch,

Who doesn't really give a stitch
For Molly Gibson's deepest feelings
But only her own darkest dealings!
She fakes her kindness and regard
And woos our Molly's dearest pa,
This idiotic stupid man
Falls for the silly woman's plan
Then weds and she becomes no other
Than Molly's wicked stepmother!

So Molly is all in a rage
And goes to stay up at The Grange,
This place is where the Hamleys live
And Lady H on her does give
Her love and strength to thus go on
And her two sons to focus on.
She wanted her for Osbourne Hamley
And then she'd be part of the family
But then the twists and catatonia
For Lady H dies of pneumonia!

Doctor Gibson tries to save her
And Molly's scorned for her behaviour
Because that Hyacinth implores
That she's rejected and ignored!
The whole thing hangs on women's rows
And men who plead with scrapes and bows,

For when we meet Miss Cynthia
Who's been somewhere like India
We find the stepmother in panic
For now there's rows - a new dynamic!

And Cynthia, cutest of girls
All frills, and spills, and rings, and pearls
Does hate her mum, and at her smirks
She says she's a determined flirt;
The jealous mother's quite enraged
Thinks Cynthia has her upstaged,
So they are constantly at war
While Molly and her dad endure
The screaming rows and crying fits
And smelling salts, and snarls, and spits.

Then one day Molly gets a letter
And then the plot becomes much better
Because this note contains a secret
And Molly learns that she must keep it.

The thing that Osbourne Hamley knows
Is that he's already betrothed
To French and catholic girl no less,
And now he does have to confess -
For he suspects his heart is weak
And if it is, then she should seek
To find his wife upon his death -
If he should take his final breath

And not just this, before he's done
He tells her that he's got a son!

My God, our Molly - what to do?!
She hides the note inside her shoe
And tells no one this little lie
And hopes to God he will not die!

The other brother Roger lad
Is quite the favourite of his dad,
But he falls violently for
That Cynthia her charms and all -
The Squire dislikes her and refuses
To let him have the girl he chooses.

Meanwhile, Cynthia has lied
Has used her vanity and pride
When she was young to promise to
A man that she'd be wedded to;
But mind she changed, and he persisted,
She got cross, strongly resisted,
He'd loaned her money, twenty pounds
Now Molly must release her bounds
By paying back this dodgy bill
When meeting him upon a hill.

But she was seen and rumour was
That she was seeing him because
She wanted to elope with him -
Which put her father in a spin!

If Molly lost her reputation
There'd be no end of speculation
She'd never wed a gentleman
Or get a handsome settlement!

Then fortune came to save her name
Relieve her from disgrace and blame,
Since only one to get his number
Was darling Harriet, Lady Cumnor -
She dressed herself and wore her crown
And flaunted Molly in the town -
The village folk were all impressed
And all the rumours were suppressed!

Meanwhile, a tragedy ensued,
Which left her dad most unamused
For Molly had not only lied
But once, because when Osbourne died
The whole French, catholic, wife affair
Came out, and made The Squire go spare!

But at the end the other Hamley -
Brother from that lovely family,
(From the beginning, lived with The Squire,
At Hamley Hall with church and spire),
His name is Roger, Osbourne's brother
Well, he approaches Molly's mother
Hyacinth, (well, step ma) who
Was devious, her daughter knew

That she was supercilious and rude
And used to think that Roger crude!

Well, he comes trumping in at last
With passioned heart all beating fast
And realises he's a wally
For all along he'd loved Miss Molly!

And then they wed and live their lives
At Hamley Hall where they reside,
And Cynthia, though quite inscrutable,
Does wed a cad, he's much more suitable!
And everyone is lastly wed,
Proclaimed their love and made their bed,
Except for Lady Harriet
Who storms off in her chariot!

So there it is, our authoress
Does past provincial life address
Through two young girls, their grace, propriety
In ironic critique of Victorian society!

The moral is in stormy waters
We must protect our wives and daughters!

LAST WILL AND
TESTAMENT

Bleak House

So Dickens' readers heads he fills
With legal wrangles, rows, and wills,
Right at the start we do find out
What one of these is all about -
But problem is the legal throng
Has been in lawyers' courts so long
That no one knows who is a ward
Nothing is set, nothing assured.

So in amongst the legal case
There's two young souls both fair of face,
One Ada Clare, one Richard Carson,
Both are bright and gay and spartan.
Oh, and there's this other one
Her name is Esther Summerson
(She is key, but we imagine
She's a travelling companion).

So this lot all arrive at court
Expecting this whole case to sort
Itself in months and be decided,
And then for life they'll be provided -
They'll get their dues by any price
In case of Jarndyce and Jarndyce,
By hook, or crook, or ink, or bill
They'll find out who is in the will!

So Mr Jarndyce takes them in
And then the story starts to spin -
He's generous and does announce
That he does live in an old bleak house.

Anyway, let's move a chapter
And back to fortunes they will capture -

When Guppy who's a legal clerk
Meets Esther, and in him a spark
Begins to catch into a flame
Our Summerson don't feel the same!
His place of work is Kenge/Carboys
But his attentions her annoys
For he's convinced he knows her face
But she wants him to give her space!

All the while there in the town
Where filth and grime is all around,
This guy called Crook who rents some rooms
To singletons and poorest grooms

One of which, a war hero
Who goes by pseudonym 'Nemo'
Takes opium, effects pernicious
And this makes dear old Crook suspicious!

So when he doesn't pay his rent
That naughty Crook who's sharp and bent
Goes in his room as poor guy sleeps
To rifle through this trunk he keeps -
But while he's there he sees his head
Is lopsided and limp - he's dead!

So Crook just grabs all that he can -
Some letters, books, off the poor dead man
And scarpers off into the night
Trying not to wake Miss Flight.
Now she's the one who lives at Crook's
She's into birds and hymns and books,
Well she suspects he's spun a ruse
Because he's drunk and stinks of booze,
And she had liked that Nemo chap
Whose name was 'Hordern' - she knew that!
But here she's just a fabricator
For blinding truth that comes much later
For there's this sweeper boy called Joe,
And he's the other one to know
That dying man, who kind and giving,
Had pitied him, tossed him a shilling.

So back to plot and it gets harder
The storyline gets twisted, darker...

There is this gent who's rich and old
And lives with wife at Chesney Wold.
He's Sir Leicester (baronet)
And she's a sort of suffragette,
She wants to get away from there
She's bored and filled with deep despair!

The housekeeper - she's Mrs Rouncewell -
Well, she knows something's up as well -
She's a son and he's called George
And he's the one that she adores,
Well he's gone off to serve the army
And everyone thinks he's quite barmy.

But back to Deadlock, she's capricious
And when her lawyer gets suspicious
About a child that had been born -
He's sharp that Mr Tulkinghorn!
Well, he compares the hand addressed
To Lady Honoria D no less -
A legal letter matches it
So he goes in and snatches it,
The worry vexes her poor head
And now she wants the lawyer dead!

She's also got this maid she hates
Hortense is French, and she awaits

The lawyer on one filthy night
And gives the callous man a fright -
You see, she has just been dismissed
From Chesney Wold and now she's pissed,
So to revenge her former lady
She gets all twisted, dark and shady
And she's got quite a staring part
And shoots the lawyer through the heart!

Lady Deadlock's not upset
But now she is the prime suspect!
So in comes this inspector guy
Called 'Bucket', who the hell knows why!
And he makes two and two make four
When seeing that the black fringe shawl
Was Lady Deadlock's apparel
That Hortense wore that night as well -
She'd tried to frame our Lady D
But she was guilty as can be!

But in between, for it was said,
That others wanted lawyer dead,
Was Captain George, the Rouncewell son
They blamed him for he had a gun,
But he was then believed by all
When they found out about the shawl!

Now back to Esther Summerson
Cos she's the real smoking gun,
She wants to know her own genetics

And in the process gets obsessive -
Then she gets taken by the plague
When Guppy finds out her past name -
It wasn't Summerson at first
But Hordern - so his mind does burst
Cos he does see that Lady D
And all her doom and misery
Comes from the fact that she had had
A baby with that Nemo cad!

So Lady D is terrified -
And she ran off and promptly died
Because she couldn't bear the shame
Of Esther finding out her name!

Meanwhile, the wards are getting stressed
That Richard chap is so obsessed,
He wants the money from the will
But stress of it just makes him ill!
He wants to marry Ada Clare
But Mr Jarndyce doesn't care,
He wants our Ada safely kept
So Richard died and Ada wept!

At the end there was no money
And here we laugh, Dickens is funny...

The case and cash was settled, done
But all the costs meant there was none!
So Richard died of filthy greed
And left our Ada grieved indeed!

But some good news does right the wrong,
Cos there's a chap, who all along
Quite fancied Esther for her mind,
Her innocence and nature kind,
And he saw more than greed and breeding
So Dickens does make us believe in
Men who love us warts and all
And don't care for our pasts at all!

The message is to always hide
Your vanity, and sneer, and pride,
To always be like Summerson -
The wise, and kind, and virtuous one!

Wuthering Heights

This one starts high on a moor
When a strange old man knocks on a door,
And his name's Lockwood, he's the lease
At Thrushcross Grange in blissful peace.

But on this night all is blown in
And he gets stranded there, snowed in,
And has to stay the night poor fool
In scary Hall and old bedroom.

And on that night his heart does sink
He doesn't sleep a single wink
For on the windowpane, he hears
A tapping sound which shakes his fears -
So he runs home all petrified
And tells the housekeeper, who cries,
'Oh God that place is really gory

Oh do sit down I'll share the story
Of love, and lust, and man's birthrights
And all that happened at Wuthering Heights!'

So she begins the history
Of how a black boy came to be
The master there at Wuthering Heights,
Through bitter love, and fits, and fights.

'It started off,' she said, 'with rage,
That Hindley boy a war did wage,
When his dear dad came back one day
With some young boy and he did say,
"This boy I have adopted and
He'll be a useful stable hand!"
When Hindley learnt he'd taken him in
He beat Heathcliff, accosted him,
And they did fight so hellishly
And all because of jealousy!

'What made it worse was our Cathy,
The daughter who was wild and sassy,
Fell in love with Heathcliff boy
And this the family annoyed,
So she went mad and quite deranged
And married the boy from Thrushcross Grange!
And he was fine with lots of wealth
And better for her mental health!
That was Edgar who lived here
Oh, he loved Cathy very dear!

64

'Meanwhile, Hindley went to school
And came back home with all these rules,
He treated Heathcliff quite unfair
So Heathcliff went completely spare!
He buggered off into the night
With Edgar's sister out of spite;
Got her pregnant, made some money
Then turned up smelling sweet as honey!

'So he did wed that sister Bella
Then he transpired an awful fella -
Hindley now had lost his cash
For he'd behaved extremely rash,
He'd gambled most of it away
And then wanted Heathcliff to stay
Cos Heathcliff'd got the money see,
So they then lived in misery
The wife with son then left the men
And that's the last we saw of them!

'So now Heathcliff has got revenge
But he wants more, so he upends
The peace at Thrushcross Grange, you see,
By gushing loving prophesies
To Cathy who is now with child
And all this makes her mind go wild,
So she goes mad and promptly dies
And Heathcliff balls and cries and cries!

'But baby lived a healthy fatty
Which also had the name of Cathy,
When she grew up and got much older
Heathcliff went and promptly told her
That his own son that Linton lad
Did fancy her which made her mad!

'So she went up to Wuthering Heights
And got locked in for several nights,
And Linton married Cathy's daughter
She ran away, but Heathcliff caught her
Her dad then died of shock and stress
And now the *whole thing* was a mess!

'For who owned what and what owned who?
Can you guess? That Heathcliff knew!
For all along the git had planned
To get his hands on all the land!

'Then weakling Linton passes out
And that's the end of him the lout!
And Cathy, mad, her head all spinning,
Falls for the boy's son from the beginning
That was Hindley's son you see...
Now are you really following me?

'He was Hareton, Heathcliff saw
The same old love he'd had before,
The outcome was just like a mirror
And Heathcliff's temper did now simmer.

He once was angry, causing harm
But now his temper was quite calm;
The end is that he got the lot -
Both Wuthering Heights and this old plot!
But in the end, he died quite crazy
In the very same room last night you stayed in!

'So now you know why you lacked sleep
It's Cathy's ghost that cannot keep
Away from Heathcliff's windowpane,
She roams the moor, he does the same,
Tormented souls beyond the grave
From sin and lust, no one could save
And in the end where Cathy lies
Was Heathcliff put whence he had died -
He was put the other side
Of Cathy, who had him denied!

'It's a classic tale of love and lust -
Of how a woman's virtue must
Be kept intact or else she gets
Embroiled in rage and then regrets -
When madness steals her head no less
When two men she tries to impress
Do tear the heart strings from the cradle
But in the end the pain is fatal!

'So keep away – that place is strange,
And stay here safe at Thrushcross Grange!'

Agnes Grey

This novel is a girl's account
Of suffering, which does amount
To leaving home in desperation
To earn her crust in education.

This comes about because her dad,
That Mr Grey, the silly lad,
Did all their dosh at once invest
Thinking he'd gain a large interest;
And this transaction did backfire
Which left them starving in the mire!
For this supposedly safe bet
Just brought forth pain and sheer regret
When merchant died in dire shipwreck
Left them in debt up to the neck!

So they were forced to scrimp and shiver
And Mum and Dad began to wither
So younger daughter Agnes she
Did come up with a plan you see -
She thought she'd get them what they need
By being one less mouth to feed!

So off she trots on snowy day,
Much to her father's deep dismay,
Cos he's ashamed and quite distressed
That she will work as a governess!
For in those days these bleak decisions
And teacher posts and base positions
Did denigrate and cause mayhem
To all of those who worked in them!

And as she goes over the brow
Of vale which she is leaving now,
She prays to God because she yearns
To see them all when she returns.

Then she arrives at Bloomfield's pile
And meets the mistress, rude and vile
And also three quite beastly children
Who will not heed although she wills them
To do their work, but she could kill them
With cyanide she longs to fill them!
For they are supercilious and rude
And she's left crying in her food.
The eldest one, a boy called Tom,

Well, he's the really vicious one
His father likes his impudence
And this augments his insolence!

Then one day as he's killing chicks
That fall from nest into some sticks
This torturing our Agnes dreads,
And throws a rock down on their heads!
You see she will not let him torture
Birds like this, so she must slaughter
Them so that they don't remain
Being tortured and in pain.

Anyway, she ups and leaves
She stays a year, but she believes
That not all families will be
Quite as rude and forthright see,
So she goes back to mother's nest
Where all that lot are poor and stressed,
And Aggie knows she must be able
To put more grub upon the table.

So she asks Mum to help her find
Another post this time with kind
And loving folk who want a teacher
Who value her and want to keep her.

So she finds folk, these Murrays who
Are looking for a missy to
Befriend and instruct daughters so

The girls will French and German know.
So she replies to said post published
To teach the girls to be accomplished,
For in those days you wouldn't bag
A fine and loaded handsome stag
Unless you weren't just fair of face
And dressed from head to toe in lace,
But also very finely bred
Exceedingly accomplished and well read!

So she arrives at Horton Lodge
But finds these girls a mess because
They have the tempers of their mum
And she's a real bitch that one,
The only one that gives a crap
Is a cute little dog by the name of Snap!

Though Agnes stays compunctious
Matilda she's rambunctious,
And other girl that Rosalie
Lacks discipline and doesn't see
That flirting looks and fans and dresses
Only rotters that impresses!
Of Agnes she cares not a tuppence
But boy does she get her comeuppance
Since she ends up with this rich dude,
Unscrupulous and really rude!

Meanwhile, Agnes goes to church
And as the wedding is rehearsed

She falls in love there with the vicar -
This Eddie chap who makes her shiver
With joy when one fine summer's day
He picks some primroses to say
With subtlety, 'I'm your disciple,'
And she does press them in her bible,
And treasures them but is quite coy;
In those days courtship with the boy
Had to be slow and tender, caring
Not like today by photo sharing!

So Agnes goes weak at the knee
But then there's a catastrophe,
Cos back at home her dad is dying
And Agnes asks for leave implying
That she would like to homeward go
But Mrs Murray she says, 'No!
Not till the holidays, you'll leave,'
Ignoring Agnes crying, 'Pleeease!'
So when they came she upped and legged it,
But when she got there, he had pegged it!
Although the carriage it had sped
When she gets home her dad is dead!

Anyway, there's tears and she
Goes back to Murrays miserably,
But Edward Weston had to go
So she's without her gorgeous beau -
The one who gave her pretty flowers
And occupied her thoughts for hours!

And misery goes on and on
When she finds out the doggie's gone,
So even more despair ensues
Much weeping, heartbreak, and tissues
And then she sees she's been obtuse
To Mrs Murray's cold abuse
And leaves at night in horse and carriage
A spinster, sad, and still unmarried.

So home she goes and says to mother,
'I'm miserable, I want a lover!'
And mum says, 'You must stay genteel,
And hide the pain inside you feel.'

With gallantry she does compose
Herself by reading tonnes of prose
And tries to keep herself refined,
With work to occupy her mind.

Then one day Agnes on her stool
Sits up and says, 'How 'bout a school
That we set up for useless brats,
I'll teach them Latin you do maths!'
The mum says, 'Yes,' and off they go
Down to the coast, a place unknown,
But quite by chance do you know who
Is also loitering there too?

Yes, on the beach there is her chap
Out walking with his doggie Snap -

The same little pooch from earlier
Who licks her face and jumps on her
And so does Edward Weston too
He flatters her and loves her through
And through some more he does all day
This simple girl called Agnes Grey!

And so the two of them aren't glum,
They triumph and live with her mum
In cosy cottage by the sea -
The tragic start ends happily!

I think Anne Brontë is insisting
The quest for love is worth persisting -
The message is: with strength and grit
When life is one big pile of shit
The tide can turn and us enthral -
For love and patience conquers all!

Madame Bovary

So, this French tale is all about
A woman's virtue, sin, and doubt
There's also romance, passion, lust
Capriciousness and breaking trust.

It starts with Emma, who lives on a farm
She's young, precocious, but not without charm,
Her mum is dead, her dad's a squire
And one fine day he does require
The help of medic man, you see
Because he's fallen from a tree
And snapped the bone there in his leg -
If he gets gangrene, he'll be dead
Because back then a fracture was
A real big deal, and bad because
They couldn't really operate,
I mean who would cooperate,

Without even an anaesthetic
Then hobblin' about on a wood prosthetic?

So Doctor Bovary swoops in
To save the man his leg and shin,
So he can walk about the lane
Without the need to use a cane.
He binds it up and makes a splint
And in no time there is no hint
That Mr Theodore had ever
Broken it, this man's so clever
This doctor chap, this great hero
Must have some prize for this great show!

So he and Doctor Bovary,
He's a widower also see,
They bond because he's saved his limb
And Emma now quite fancies him,
So Mr Theodore allows
The two of them to make their vows...

But almost from the wedding day
She thinks he's boring, maybe gay
Because there's not one hint of lust
No romance, passion, only dust!
This bores the gal, he is a prig
She cares for him not one damn fig!
And when they start to live together
He's always working, boring fella -

She's trapped in agoraphobia,
Develops melancholia!

So she's now crying every hour,
Depression comes and does devour,
And Bovary is none the wiser -
He's repressed, the useless miser,
So he can't really spark her fire
And she drowns further in the mire.

Then one day comes an invitation
Which stirs her from her consternation,
A ball in town which takes her fancy -
A chance to practice sycophancy!

So off they go one night in carriage
And Doc thinks this will save his marriage,
But quite reverse the outcome is
When Emma spies the rich marquis!
She dances with him gay and bright
And revels in romance all night.

So she is blissful, and now sees
The cause of all her miseries
Is being married to the doc -
The soulless, lifeless, useless crock!

But one day with his small perception
The doc decides on new election -

A situation more in town
Where she can flaunt her lacy gown
To give the girl what she does need -
Satisfaction for her greed!

So off they go to Yonville see
But this compounds his misery
For when one day this cripple comes
He unsuspectingly becomes
A project for doc's fascination -
For surgery is his vocation!

So in comes this poor Hypolyte -
Who at the first is all delight
Cos he thinks he will walk again
When club foot's cured and free from pain -
But doc does bodge the operation
Which only ends in amputation,
And this causes a denigration
And screws Doc Bovary's reputation!

So there is panic, and amid
This chaos, Emma's birthed a kid,
But this does not now help her cause
Since for it she feels zip at all -
Between the birth and doctor's folly
She slides back into melancholy!

Then disaster - heaven knows!
For at the agricultural show
Is dashing Mr Boulanger,
Who flatters her and strokes her hair -
So she gets giggly and flirtatious
But he's a bad'un quite salacious,
He takes her riding on her horse
And beds her in the woods of course!

So she's now got this wild affair
And comes back with dishevelled hair,
But still the hubby don't suspect,
He's ignorant, no self-respect!

So she goes on with wildest fling
Blind to the mayhem it will bring,
Cos when Boulanger's faithful promise
To treat her like a saintly goddess
Turns out to be just blatant lies,
She falls apart and cries and cries!

You see, they'd planned to flee together
He bottles it, leaves her a letter,
He dumps her by pathetic note
And he's revealed the useless bloke
He is, you see, they're all the same
They take the woman's heart, then blame

Society and regulations
For their own sexual frustrations!

So he sods off and leaves her weeping
And duncey doc just leaves her sleeping -
He just thinks that she's depressed
My God he's thick and so repressed!

Let's move along and get much farther
Unto the end of this whole saga –

After several fainting fits
Our Emma seems to get to grips
With life again, and does resign
Herself to her cross-stitch design...

But in a bid to quash her longings
Her empty soul craves more belongings,
And to her shame and sheer discredit
She buys this furniture on credit.
This she does with no regret
And saddles Bovary with debt.
He's so stupid, meek, oblivious
So she gets greedy, supercilious,
And then her lust reveals itself
That Emma just can't help herself!

Then she goes off to opera halls
At Rouen, and there in the stalls
Is this young chap Léon, indeed
She'd known him all along you see –

Anyway, he is quite cute,
And Bovary's still so aloof,
She thinks, *oh well I need amusing*
This lad with floppy hair's worth schmoozing!

So off she jumps into a carriage
Without a care left for her marriage
And Léon ravishes the tart
And falls for her with all his heart,
But by this point her chilling soul
Is withered, cursed, and frozen cold,
And all she wants is for him to
Pay off the debts she did accrue.
So when it dawns on her he's brassic
And gushy, needy, and dramatic,
She dumps the boy and runs back to
The guy who made her glum and blue!

And this time all she needs is cash
So she pleads love, but's rather brash,
And Mr Boulanger once more
Rejects her, she falls to the floor
With broken heart – a withered crow
From all this dollar she does owe!

So near the end she does decide
That she's possessed and cursed with pride,
So she elects to kill herself
With poison from the doctor's shelf.
So she chugs down some arsenic
Which makes her green and really sick,
And after days of brutal wailings
And misery from all her failings
She pops her clogs, her days now spent
But not before she does repent -
With one last breath she gets the priest -
Confesses, and her mind's released!

The doc indeed he is quite nice
For though he's thick, he's paid the price
For wedding the old flibbertigibbet
But no regrets, not for a minute!

It's there we see in this last part
That constancy in love's the art -
For who of us could have predicted
That he'd forgive the sin inflicted?!

But this he does and then at end
We sort of like the doctor's trend
For honesty and trust in God,
But still he is a stupid sod!

The moral is that wedded bliss
Can be a curse if you do kiss
A frog, a toad, a dashing prince
Or any man, both then and since -
So women you must only bind
Yourselves to men who good and kind
Do constant stay, but also find
A boy that stimulates your mind!

Northanger Abbey

This one's cute, to be read in a day
About a young girl who is pretty and gay,
She's called Catherine Morland see
She's sheltered, kind, and sweet sixteen -
Never been kissed, or heard, or seen,
And bored of the cross-stich and housework routine!

Anyway, she's one of many
And she's not got the time for any-
-Thing but washing kids and clothes
Occasional reading, fiction, prose,
And this is important because she's impressed
By mythical goblins which makes her obsessed!

This comes about from Udolpho
(That was a scandalous book you know),
Which gave our Cathy quite a shock,
And made her go silly and gothic, baroque,
For what made Udolpho even more shady
Was that it was scribed by an infamous lady!

Anyway, our Catherine lass
Well, she's unworldly and she lacks
Comportment, grace, and education,
So one fine day to her elation
The Allens, who live near her folks,
Suggest she needs to meet some blokes
So they're like, 'Come to Bath with us!'
And she's like, 'Yay, indeed!' because
She's desperate for some entertainment
And longs for a boy and a swift engagement!

So, Mr Allen, he's got gout
And that's what he is all about
And Mrs Allen wants an excursion
And he could quite do with a bit of diversion!

So off they go in horse and carriage
With hopes and dreams of balls and marriage,
They get to Bath and all is fine
And Cath is expecting to have a great time...

But then at the ball as they're smiling politely
There's no one familiar, not even slightly
So the Allens are like, *'We've got no acquaintance!'*
But Cath's got the boys under closest surveillance!

So when they leave The Upper Rooms
A meeting with this boy ensues,
When Mrs Allen's lace and pin
Gets tangled up and stuck to him,
And he's like, 'Oh my dear you need
Some help in order to be freed!
Oh, is this fine sprigged muslin I
Have seen in fancy shops nearby?!'

And Mrs Allen, fond of lace,
Gets all obsessed because his face
Is handsome and he compliments
Sprigged muslin from the continent!

So she's all giggly, quite enraptured,
And Cathy's pleased because she's captured
Fortune from enquiry -
Something to write in her diary!

Then she finds out his name is Tilney
And hopes he'll court, pursue, but will he?

And then by chance, for who would have thought,
They meet Mrs Allen's old friend Mrs Thorpe!
She's got daughters similar in age

To Cathy, which means that they're on the same page;
All looking for men to seduce and enamour
Impress with their language, their wit, and their grammar!

The oldest one is Isabella -
She's a looker and out for a fella
With money, and status, and all those fine things,
She dresses in jewels, and bracelets, and rings
She's a terrible snob and a social climber
But Cathy's naïve so she doesn't mind her!

So, they get pally and go to buy books
And there's these two boys who start shooting them looks
And Cathy's embarrassed, all churlish and shy -
But Isabella isn't, and do you know why?

Well, that's because she is a tease
Pursuing the boys with weakened knees,
This goes on and Cathy at first
Thinks she is great and then she does burst
With fits of giggles, flirtation, and laughter,
Leading her into impending disaster;
For when Izzy's brother that John rocks up,
He almost immediately cocks up
Cos he tells Tilney's General pa
That she is an heiress from Leamington Spa!

Right, so that's the scene all set,
But let's address and not forget
That with John Thorpe is Cathy's brother -
He's called James and he's the other
Character who's quite significant
Cos he fancies Izzy and thinks she's magnificent!

Then one day Cath meets Eleanor,
A charming girl who impresses her.
She's the Tilney's sister see
And she takes a liking and asks with a plea
If Cathy will go for a walk with them to
Admire the lakes and the hills that they knew.

So she's like, 'Yay!' cos this is a chance
To impress Mr Tilney, his love to enhance,
But that idiot boy John Thorpe's also after
Cathy's fair hand and so he does ask her
To jump in the phaeton with him because
He has decided to go to Wick Rocks
With Izzy and James, but he's superficial
He lyingly says that to make it official
For his sister to be in a carriage with men
That she'll have to come and accompany them!

So Cathy goes off at speed with John Thorpe
And jibs from her date with the Tilneys of course,
And then when she sees them right there on their feet
Walking with haste along Argyle Street,
The Tilneys assume that our Cathy is rude

And Thorpe just protests that she's being a prude
And she's like, *'You idiot stop the carriage,*
You bugger you've ruined my prospects of marriage!'
When she cries hysterical, *'I must say sorry!'*
He tells her she's silly and she shouldn't worry!

The Tilneys forgive her so that's okay
And they go for a walk on the very next day,
Mr Tilney, she finds out is Henry
His knowledge of poetry's not elementary;
He understands the plot of Udolpho
And this does elate our dear Cathy you know,
Cos she thinks gothic love's fantastic
(Austen's being so sarcastic!)

Meanwhile, our dear old friend Isabella
Well, she's busy schmoozing the brother fella -
That silly James boy falls for her plan
To capture the bugger and make him her man!

But when she sees that he's no dollar
And she'll have to slum it with him in squalor,
She backtracks a bit and leaves him hanging
He goes to Oxford his heart and soul panging!

Then Tilneys decide that since Cathy's rich
(Or so they've been told by that John Thorpe bitch)
That she should spend more time with them
So they get much closer of course, but by then
At this point our Cathy's gone a bit crabby
But she gets invited to Northanger Abbey!

At first they have a grand old time
Touring the castle and swigging down wine,
But the dad is quite formal and starts getting odd
So Cathy imagines a murder, because
She's read Udolpho when she was a teen,
And she then decides that his wife must have been
Killed by him, and with this intimation
Henry goes wild with a curt protestation,
And he gets capricious with dear Catherine
Which puts the poor wretch in a terrible spin!

Meanwhile, back in Bath their brother
The Captain Fredrick Tilney no other,
Has seduced our flaunting Izzy see
Then dumped her causing misery,
So her reputation is getting no better,
So she takes her quill and writes a letter
To Cathy at Tilneys' castle see
Asking for James's forgiveness, but she
Does see Isabella's true colours at last
And decides that with Izzy she just can't be arsed!

But right at that moment the General Tilney
Makes Cathy cry out with shame until she
Is booted and banished from Northanger Abbey,
For being so stupid and thoughtless and blabby.

Alone she does travel for days and for nights,
Ashamed of her blunders, the fall outs and fights,
And when she gets home, she vows to let go
Of reading wild literature like Udolpho!

Then a few weeks later who does show up?
But Tilney, the romance could make one throw up!
And he is ashamed of his father's behaviour
And he is the hero, the lover, and saviour
So he says, 'Dear Catherine, even though poor
I'll take you, and love you, it's you I adore!
For everyone cares for their riches, estates,
But I only care for amending mistakes!'

So Henry goes mushy and down on one knee
And Cathy is smitten and happy you see –

I guess what Miss Austen has cleverly shown
Is the *person's* important and not what they own,
But even though ending is sealed with a kiss
It's obvious Austen is taking the piss
Cos right from beginning, the novel entire
Is dripping with wit and social satire!

Middlemarch

This study of provincial life
Is full of passion, grief, and strife
But also God, political drama,
Remorse, revenge, justice, and karma.

It starts when a doctor with hopes and ideas,
Who's studied in Paris, outdoing his peers,
Arrives in the town with notions of progress -
Where townsfolk are simple and just couldn't know less
About reform, the future aim,
Their ignorance is what's to blame,
Those Middle English simple minds
Are all a bit behind the times
You know, and that's the reason why
He's here you see, he wants to try
To lift them up through this endeavour -
He's a bright young fella and rather clever.

Next let's introduce estates -
There's three of them and this creates
A sort of triangle around
That middle English market town.
One is Lowick, one Tipton Grange
The other's name is rather strange,
Don't laugh or ever try to split
This name of place they call 'Freshitt'
Or you'll digress, find you've forgot
The complex nature of the plot!

Anyway, let's start at Lowick
Where lives this man who's weird and stoic -
But also rude and supercilious,
Scrupulous minded and punctilious.
He's the scholar Casaubon
In academia he's shone,
He's scribing these anthologies
'The key to all mythologies'
And he gets asked to Tipton Grange,
What happens next is rather strange
For there's this young girl Dorothea
And she becomes his panacea,
Since she's all holy, good as thou
And he's like, 'Ah my luck's in now,'
For he's been after someone diligent
With intellect; refined, resilient,
To gather all these frantic scribings
To more intelligible writings.

Her uncle Mr Arthur Brooke -
An aristo but quite the crook,
Well, he means well but tenants listed
Live poorly cos he's so tight-fisted!

Then Doro's sister, she's called Kitty,
She's vacuous and not as pretty,
She's into this James Chettam dude
But at the start he seems quite rude.
He's got money, rotundas, palladiums
And she's into babies and fond of geraniums -
Well, when Sir James who lives at Freshitt,
Loses Miss D and has to forget it
He goes for Kitty, grabbing her hands
And they exchange their wedding bands...

Right, that's them, but now I'll mention
Casaubon's cousin, who has the intention
To raise himself from mystery,
Rewrite his chequered history.
For his old granny, she had made
Unfortunate marriage and ended a maid
Without a jot of cash you see,
So he's got a plan to reclaim and retrieve -
He's very handsome and called Ladislaw
And he hates his uncle and thinks he's a bore.

Now to the town and provincial folk -
I'll start with this useless Freddy bloke
Well, he's called Vincy, he's obsessed

With a girl in the village who's rather repressed,
She's called Garth and christened Mary
Fred wants her, but she's a bit wary
He's unscrupulous, unreliable
Gambling sort and mind is pliable,
Bit of a trader, sells the odd horse
Which always turns out a disaster of course!

He's got a sister Rosamunde Vincy
She likes piano, Leonardo da Vinci,
And after lots of swings and turns
And tears, and rants, and scorns, and spurns,
Dr Lydgate can't ignore
That she's the one he does adore.
So they get hitched in swathes of bliss
But then things start to go amiss...

Back to Fred, he's airy fairy
And he's got his heart set on Miss Mary,
But he's in debt and thinks he'll still
Recoup the funds from his uncle's will -
The fortune's Mr Featherstone's
And Mary works at the house he owns.
That's the one that Fred intends
To live in whence his fate amends
With fortune and his rightful dues
And then Miss Mary will him choose.

Back to plot and Dorothea
(You know, who wed that bore to free 'er

From binds of uncle at Tipton Grange
And took that supercilious and strange
And weird old bloke, that Casaubon,
Who's always preaching, banging on),
Well, she's getting bored and woefully dubious
Cos Casaubon's dull and doleful, lugubrious,
So when they're in Rome on a spring vacation,
She's sick of the miser, in writhing frustration,
And while she's parading enjoying bohemia
And he's in the Biblioteca Accademia -
Being virtuous, apostolic
And constantly driving Doro neurotic -
She meets by chance our Ladislaw
Whose ears prick up, but she's not sure,
And she does there encounter him
While drying her eyes at the Trevi Fountain.

Back in Middlemarch and things are progressing -
There's death, and lies, and secrets confessing;
And when old Featherstone's heart gives out
The funeral's done, and the will's read out -
Fred is denied his grand accumulation,
But rather than enhancing in Mary's estimation
This only removes him from her acceptance,
For she don't respect this Freddy's dependence
On money; she'd like him to be presciendent,
And work honestly to become independent.

Back with Doro, she's at Lowick,
She's miserable but doesn't show it,

Casaubon's screaming, and she's scribing quick,
Wishing to God to escape from this prick,
His heart is fading, his health isn't great
But he's so conniving and gets more irate
And hints while she's scrubbing and doing the dishes
That in his demise she should uphold his wishes,
She's all confused, annoyed, filled with dread
But then in the morning Casaubon's dead!

Right, you got it? That's most of the first bit,
Then it gets twisted and really immersive!

Now for Bulstrode, he's the banker -
He is a knob and a bit of a wanker!
When Fred was diddled from Stone Court
The townsfolk were seething cos Bulstrode had bought
This redolent place and made it his own,
But slowly the truth of his character's shown,
For though he is rich, he's also shady
Cos he took the funds of a curious lady -
She disappeared; was assumed she was dead
But she was alive, and he knew, but instead
Of confessing that she was in good health,
He kept schtum and ran off with her wealth.
He's a gargantuan contradiction
Cos he's always prophesising benediction!

He's important, but for now
Back to Lydgate and his row
With Rosamunde (for he is Tertius)

And things go askew when she gets discourteous;
First when Cousin Lydgate stays
And leads our Rosamunde astray,
She's with child and meant to be resting,
But the cousin is wild and always protesting
That a Countess he knows was opposed to refinement
To sitting around in her childbirth confinement,
So he grabs the saddles, starts pulling the girth,
Tells Rosie to ride right up to the birth,
So though she's been told that at home she must stay
She flatly refuses and goes anyway!

Off she gallops along with her matey
And promptly falls off and loses the baby!
So Cousin Lydgate, he's sent packing,
But the other disaster is they're now lacking
Dollar, because the doctor's profession
Ain't paying which leads to a doleful succession
Of losses, and bills, and humiliation -
Which Rosamunde feels is a gross degradation!

She's ceaselessly moaning and rueing cost cut,
Constantly screaming and doing his nut
His honourable intentions and gratuitous time
Ain't earning a penny, not even one dime,
If they don't find dollar then they'll lose their lodgings
He wants her supporting, but she blames his bodgings!

Back to Doro, she's in mourning
But the will's read out, and she's left scorning
Casaubon, cos he did leave
A codicil, which makes her grieve -
In event of his death this sinister law
States she cannot marry Will Ladislaw...

So she's now worried that everyone thinks
That she's been flirtatious and giving him winks,
But this isn't true for she'd always been missus
Devoted to Casaubon, stuck to his wishes,
So she's now in anguish, thin as a rake -
Cross with the husband and losing her faith!

Back to Bulstrode, he's being bribed
By this filthy old drunk who arrives as described;
He knows the truth that his wealth was accrued
By falsest pretence and he wants him screwed
Over, you see, so he stoops to malfeasance
Trying his patience and testing his credence...

So when Dr Lydgate inspects the old skunk,
Who's dying in bed and hopelessly drunk,
He tells Mr Bulstrode to not give him liquor
Or else he will suffer and die much quicker -
So Bulstrode decides that he'll offer doc money
He's smarmily generous, sweet as honey,
So doctor accepts, then can't understand
Why the drunk sod then dies and couldn't withstand
What he thought was a fever, mild liver disease

But Bulstrode's given him whiskey to cease
The felon, who snuffs it and Bulstrode is pleased
Cos his secret's safe and now he is freed!

So though all this stress does his wife aggrieve
They pack their belongings and up sticks and leave,
And now he's remorseful, riddled with guilt,
Suspicion now rising right up to the hilt,
But leaving The Court to his nephew Fred
Will put right injustice and put it to bed.
So Fred's now all gushy, raptured and noble
And Mary accepts his marriage proposal!

But Lydgate is doubted and his reputation
Is under the hammer from wild speculation,
But Doro, well she knows the doctor's all right -
So she sticks her neck out and puts up a fight,
And cos she's respected, she calms speculation
And rescues his name from this false accusation!

Rosie is thrilled and thanks Dorothea
Their gaff is removed from the auctioneer,
And Rosie, well she also knows that our Will
Is deeply in love with our Dorothy still.
So cos she's all pally with Will Ladislaw
She tells Dorothea it's her he adores.

So right at the end our brave Dorothea
Chucks in the fortune and Ave Marias
And chooses to marry that Will Ladislaw -
For love and not money - *to hell with the law!*

The point to it all and why it's so thrilling,
Is love conquers all if you're ready and willing
To ditch posh convention and make sacrifice,
And throw it all in for the love of your life!

Brideshead Revisited

This one's poetic, an epic, a blinder,
Protagonist's dashing by name of Charles Ryder.
At the beginning we're in World War Two
And he's disillusioned and totally through
With war, and fights, and strict army life,
With orders, commands, with death and with strife;
But by changeful events they have to move fast
And he goes to a place that he's known from his past.
So when he arrives, forlorn and dispirited,
He's astonished to find that it's Brideshead revisited!
This is the place where he's loved and he's lost
Broken his heart and paid a great cost!

And then our Evelyn spills the truth
In former memories of youth;
When Charles was in Oxford, history reading
With dashing young chaps all fair, of fine breeding -

One of which is a fine-looking dandy
He's floppy and fair and a bit of eye candy,
But though he's a looker, he's rather contrite,
Eccentric and odd is Sebastian Flyte!
He's edgy and bright, but also capricious
And constantly clutching this bear Aloysius!

He's got two sisters, one's got anaemia
The elder one's Julia, she is Cordelia,
His father's a Marchmain and he is a lord
Likes smoking and drinking and being abroad.
Lady Theresa, well she's marchioness,
She's catholic, devoted, and rather obsessed,
Questionably forthright, acrimonious
She's constantly priggish and sanctimonious,
And when she's not preaching and being the martyr
She's condemning the drunk and cheating father!

All of this chaos, well this all amounts
To Sebastian's rebellious drinking bouts!

So one fine day in their freshers' year
Seb goes out and gets hammered on beer,
He stumbles right into Charlie's front door
And promptly pukes up all over the floor!
Charlie is horrified, who is that prick
With teddy in hand that's just been sick?!

Next day our Seb, well he's all remorseful
Feels so ashamed that he gets resourceful,
Invites our Charlie out for the day
He's charming, and handsome, and witty, and gay -
I don't mean happy, I mean *gay*
A homo, queer, and bent, *that way!*

When Charlie discerns that his mind does bend
And he steers the punt from the Cambridge end,
He sort of falls in love with him
He's wild, creative, suave, and slim.

They drink and smoke and ramble, spill,
Reciting poetry on Boars Hill.
They ought to be reading in Bodleian Library
Debating philosophy eruditely
But they're obsessed with hedonism
Which leads to heavy criticism,
Though they care not and party till dawn
Debauched behaviour becoming the norm!

And as this affair proceeds to enhance
Charles meets the eccentric Anthony Blanche,
So now there's a tribe of irregular folk
And they all get sozzled and drink and smoke.

Then Seb decides to flaunt the affair
So they jump in the car with the teddy bear,
They go down to Brideshead, Seb wailing, perverse,
To meet Nanny Hawkins, his nursery nurse.

His puerile, fatuous, childish manner
Makes Charlie question and splutter and stammer,
But this all pails when Charlie does see
The beauty of Brideshead, its great majesty -
A gargantuan pile, a real stately home
Bigger than Blenheim and grander than Stowe!

Charlie's in raptures, eyes out on stalks
Gazing at Seb and in riveting talks,
But soon they must leave for Nanny does say
That Julia Marchmain is coming to stay -
She is the sister, she's also quite fine
But Seb is insistent they don't have the time!

So Seb runs off, jumps in the Bentley
Despises his family evidently,
And Charlie does ask him if he is ashamed
And Seb is all anguished; it's them that he blames -
According to him they just drink Beaujolais
And are constantly taking his things away,
Charlie then thinks that Seb's paranoid
And sees that his upbringing has him destroyed,
It's obvious now that his being gay
Will upset his family, bring them dismay!

Then off they trot to ramble in Venice
Where the father is flirting and being a menace
With his mistress you see, which causes more mayhem,
And the parents, well Charlie he starts to blame them
For Seb's debauched and drunken behaviour
But he thinks his love will be Sebbie's own saviour!

Back in Oxford behaviour gets worse,
They flunk their exams and in drinking immerse,
Seb's being taken by forces of evil
Spewing his guts up by Christchurch Cathedral;
He carries on drinking expensive champagne,
Chucking inheritance right down the drain -
Charlie calms down, he's much more wise
But Seb just keeps drinking, which is his demise -
Getting hammered's a hold on him
The whisky he craves and the outcome's grim!

Then Lady Marchmain being a catholic
Comes up to Oxford going spastic,
Telling Charles to stop Seb drinking,
But how can he stop him, and what is she thinking?
He's out of control, and she's being mean
And decides that the lush will now live with the dean -
She hopes he will drum in some good moderation,
Making him study, improve concentration,
She thinks this will make him mend silly ways
Ignoring the fact that Sebastian's gay!

But Seb just resents the control of this geezer,
And when he gets hammered and blottoed at Easter
He's sent off abroad with an Oxford don
But the miserable lush is just too far gone!

Meanwhile, Charles, he sods off to France
To get over Seb, his career to advance,
He's disillusioned, in lovesick malice
Wandering aimlessly around Paris.

Meanwhile, Seb, well he's still rebelling,
Escaping the don who's constantly yelling,
And when they return to England again
Charles is delighted to see his old friend.

But this time the mother is praying for Seb
Crossing herself for his life but instead
Of changing his ways or dearly repenting
He gets more morose and disdainful, lamenting!

The mother is hopeless and wailing and grunting
And when he decides to take a day's hunting
She stops his allowance, so he's not a dime
To indulge in the boozy, debauched pastime,
So Charles gives him money at mother's disgust
And she thinks he's cruel and broken her trust!

So she sends him packing and Seb doesn't care
He's done with control and she's a nightmare,
Charles thinks the mother is breaking his soul
By denying him money, increasing control!

If only they'd let him do as he wished -
A gay boy with teddy, flamboyant, rakish,
Then Seb wouldn't feel the need to rebel
But all of this flops and he plunges to hell!

So he sods off, disappears abroad;
Marchmains' disgusted and clearly floored,
Charles doesn't think that he'll ever return
To Brideshead, but one day his ears do burn
When Julia Marchmain calls up on the blower
Says mother is dying, and now that she's lower
She's less superficial and more understanding,
Remorseful, and thinks that Charles' longstanding
Relation with Seb could help him to see
The error he's made, and with desperate plea
She asks him to bring our Seb to her side
But Seb doesn't want to, and she promptly dies!

Seb's in Morocco, he's in a hospice
He's moaning, delirious, clearly lost it,
Shacked up with a gay boy, a German called Kurt
Who's also a drunk, and a waster, a burk.
So they are determined to do as they please,
Smoking and coughing and dying of greed,
The situ is hopeless and Charles leaves him there,

Seb is indifferent and just doesn't care!

Years go by and Charles gets hitched
To a pretty young thing, but a bit of a bitch,
Now Julia's wed but he's in touch with Cordelia,
Denounces his gayness and marries this Celia -
She's into diamonds and parties exotic
A social climber and slightly neurotic!

They're leaving New York, where he's been painting
And get the boat back but she's constantly fainting,
The voyage is long and she's in the cabin,
She's seasick and spewing her guts up and gagging,
And Julia's there, she's escaping the hubby
(That Rex bloke she's worked out's inconstant and grubby),
So she pours her heart out to Charlie re Rex
And they tear all their clothes off and start having sex!

Celia's boring so he chucks her in
Moves in with Julia, living in sin,
Father is dying and while he's repenting
Julia goes most devout and lamenting -
Says she can't marry him now and she prays -
She knows he's inconstant and swings both ways!

So that is the end of Charles Ryder's tale,
An interesting insight to the life of a male
Who gets all confused and really done in
By sister and brother, religion, and sin,
Embroiled with a family, complex and bigoted -
It's all to be found there in Brideshead Revisited!

Thus Spake Zarathustra

This one's more an allegory
To place in its own category;
Scribed by a wild and wonderful creature,
The madman (or genius) Friedrich Nietzsche!

Inspired by rising anarchism
He wrote in prose and aphorism.
Some state his mind polluted
Since writing's convoluted
Some even say egregious
But I think him ingenious!

His writing's wild and I did find
It swept me up and blew my mind,
His insight was so frightening
But also most enlightening!

It starts with a guy who's sick of society,
Done with the binds of religious piety,
So Zarathustra, that's his name
Is after freedom, that's his game,
Averse to people, pointless outings,
He packs his bag; encamps in the mountains -
He's up there a decade dissecting religion,
Unfurling his mind and increasing his wisdom.

But one day at breakfast, there in his cave
He looks at the sky with a rant and a rave;
'I'm weary of wisdom, just like a bee
I've got too much honey and this I decree:
I must share my knowledge, I've pondered and written
The truth of existence, but will people listen?!'

So then he descends and finds this old saint -
Devoted to God but a wise man he ain't!
He's done with the town and from people he's fleeing
But who is this chap from the mountains he's seeing?

And Zara is raging and blabbing till red
And shouts at the saint, 'Don't you know God is dead?!'
What Zara has learnt and what he has worked out
Is that being a hero is what it's about!

This is the Übermensch, great superman,
Who conquers himself through a break from the clan.
He's gallant, heroic, courageous, and bold,
He'll triumph from illness and turn muck to gold!

He's someone intrepid with great fortitude,
Who learns to be wise in prolonged solitude -
You see, to gain freedom and doctrines disown
Is only achievable when he's alone!

Onwards with story and Zara's all down,
The saint didn't listen, so on to the town,
And he is determined that these stupid dopes
Should trust in themselves and not heavenly hopes!

And there in the square does he try as seducer
But no one will listen to our dear Zarathustra...

Then out of the blue there's a tightrope walker
Attempting to cross from restraint to the altar.
He loses his grip, and the crowd holds their breath
And the tightroper stumbles and falls to his death,
In metaphor Nietzsche does wish us to see
Importance of crossing to set yourself free -
There's danger in crossing to lift consciousness
But risk must be taken to reach providence!

So he says to the walker who fell on his head,
'You died for an honour, even though God is dead!'
He sits with the corpse and praises his glory,
Then buries his body, goes on with the story.

But Zarathustra begins to see
That waking the herd will not be easy.
He sees that the masses are blind and obsessed

With societies' doctrines, theological texts,
So he thinks it's better to get single types
To follow his teachings and with this he hypes
Them up with these stories with which he will channel
Them into his teachings and starts with the camel.

The camel is strong and carries the weight,
Just like the human who wrestles his fate,
Then on to a lion who'll roar in defence
As humans must fight for their independence!

The lion then fights with the serpent who tries
To catch him, and kill him, and eat him alive.
The human's the same with political rules,
Which stop him creating his own values!

If the lion succeeds in his mission to beat
The serpent and force him to flee and retreat,
Then this leads to liberty, autonomy,
And then he has retrieved his freedom you see!

The lion destroys all these values conventional
And now lives a life more authentic, intentional,
This genius allegory intends we become
A sage and a prophet - A Superhuman!
Then metamorphose to the eyes of a child
Who's innocent, loving, free-thinking but mild,
And this overcoming, well this does create
The person who's free, in control of his fate!

The way to autonomy's being alone,
In solitude so that the human can own
His self and his morals, his principles too,
If he can achieve this, then he'll find it's true,
He'll will his own will, not be cursed by a body
Of brainwashing, lies, and corruption so godly!

Then Nietzsche explains the flaw of compassion
Which only breeds sheep who regorge parrot-fashion -
Example he gives is in loving thy neighbour
Cos how does this pitying pious behaviour
Allow him to conquer misguided believing,
Promote superhuman, advance his achieving?

The other debate is that dear Jesus Christ
Who took to the cross sacrificing his life
Did do so too early before he had learnt
To embrace life for living and loving the earth;
He's telling us not to anticipate death
As the bible does preach, but to save us our breath
And let us live lives that are rich, full of joy,
Without the constrictions these doctrines employ!

Create obligation and this will prevent
People from rising, but wail and lament,
The wise man goes further, equality's useless,
Superhumans aren't equal - they're brave and they're ruthless!

The call for equality comes from those who
Have herd-like mentalities, envious too,
The will to true power comes from being strong
Overcoming the self and undoing the wrong,
Through suffering, pain, and then wisest reflection
Comes triumph and wisdom through deep introspection!

And when you do free yourself, you'll know no longer
Constriction, control; and your *self* will be stronger!

Anna Karenina

This finest tale of Russian gentry,
Considered the best of the nineteenth century,
Imbues the tale of a love affair
With religion, politics, and despair -
Richly portrayed in Russian society
With scrutinisation of God almighty!

It starts with a prince, he's called Oblonsky,
He's high and he's mighty, he's pompous and poncy.
He's just been caught in an awkward folly
When playing around and cheating on Dolly.
She is the wife, and she is depressed
Cos hubby's been shagging the governess!

She wants divorce, but he wants forgiveness,
She's going mental, and he's losing interest
But Stiva's a plan – that's his nickname -

So he writes to his sis of Karenina fame.
She is called Anna, and she is the lead,
She's highly accomplished and it is agreed
That she is the prettiest girl in all Russia -
She's dressed to the nines and plastered in blusher.

So Anna rocks up at the railway station
And there's this hot guy and a wild flirtation,
Instant attraction like honey to bee
When Anna runs into this Count Vronsky;
She's been chatting, seducing his mother,
Who's rocking with laughter, so she is another
To fall for Anna's grace and propriety -
She's wildly attractive in Russian society!

But Vronsky is in the heart of a pretty
Youngish fine girl by the name of Miss Kitty,
But he is a player, a bit of a liar
Which hurts little Kitty Shcherbatskaya!

There's also a guy called Konstantin Levin,
But he's far too obvious, pleadin' and beggin',
So she's not really into him
And hopes that Vronsky's love she'll win;
But he's obsessed with Anna now
But she's a married wife, the cow,
So Kitty scowls and disapproves
And everybody's unamused.

So that is how they're all related
And here's how the mayhem is created...

The following night there is this big ball
And passion's alighted between them all;
When Kitty sees Vronsky and Anna in waltz
There's a realisation that his love is false,
And as she looks on as they fondly embrace
A sadness descends on her pitiful face...

She loses her heart and her head for a lover
And is whisked to a German spa to recover.

Meanwhile, Anna is torn with remorse
And gets on a train to go home, but of course
Vronsky is smitten and wildly obsessed
So he's at the station trying his best
To get her to stay and give up her marriage,
Elope with him, run away in a carriage...

But she can't bear to leave her son
So she says, 'No,' with him she's done -
But now she's constantly depressed;
The husband knows, and he is stressed.
They row and fight for weeks on end -
How can this frightful rift now mend?

Vronsky won't leave it and he does persist
And Anna attempts to retreat and resist,
But she is so horny she loses her head
And they wildly screw on his four-poster bed!

She has now fallen headlong for The Count
But this reckless behaviour well this does amount
To scandal and gossip at horse racing spectacle
Which Russian society deems unacceptable!

Then Anna tells Vronsky that she is expecting -
Right before race, so he is reflecting,
Not thinking about the race on his horse -
And he goes a crasher right there on the course!

Karenin is watching as Anna goes mad,
She's worried for Vronsky and terribly sad,
So he goes ballistic, and slaps her a bit,
And she throws a tantrum and calls him a shit.

Meanwhile, Levin is sad to hear Kitty
Is tragically dying and thinks it's a pity,
But she has befriended this girl who believes her
And goes by the name of Varvara Andreevna.
They become pally at this German spa
And Kitty gets better and stronger by far.

Meanwhile, Anna does nothing but cry,
Cos she's had a dream that she will soon die,
And Vronsky's shocked and goes quite blue
Cos he's had the same premonition too -
So they're in a mess and she's going mad
And the whole situation is desperately bad!

Meanwhile, Levin's decided he will
Propose to our Kitty, for he loves her still,
So at the Oblonskys while they are all dining
He asks for her hand, and she's finally smiling.

So they get wed and now she is free
From heartbreak, and curses, and sheer misery.

But Vronsky is cross because he has lost
Career, and respect, and paid a great cost
For Anna, who's wed with a bastard baby,
He's doing his nut but thinks that maybe
If only Karenin would grant a divorce,
Then Anna and him could resume intercourse!

But this is delusion, a folly, a whim
And Anna is dying, her head in a spin -
She's got a fever in her lying-in
And husband is crying, forgiving her sin!

But Anna recovers - she aims to stay,
Religion does win and she cannot betray
Her husband, who *doesn't* grant the divorce
And Vronsky then loses *his* mind of course!

So he gets a gun and points at his heart
But misses and smashes his torso apart!
But somehow he lives and now wants to flee
With Anna, so they run to Italy.

Meanwhile, Levin is questioning, doubting
His faith and his marriage as Kitty's now shouting.
But then when his brother is breathing his last
Kitty is tender and strong to the last -
This quiet display of fond dedication
Increases her virtue in his estimation.

Back in St Petersberg, Vronsky and Anna
Return, but reception is cold and the manner
Towards them is hatred, for they are outcast,
For degrading behaviour and sinful past.
Vronsky now thinks she's a terrible mother
So they start chastising, resenting each other.

And when they return to their friends in Moscow
(Since all comes out in the wash you know),
Anna charms Levin, which makes Kitty cross,
Vronsky goes wild and anticipates loss,
His mother suggests that he marries a princess -
She's called Sorokin, but he has no interest

But Anna now jealous, and totally mad
Is downing the morphine, and it's getting bad!
She suddenly sees that she can't make this work
She's totally lost it and going berserk -
So amid all the tears, the heartbreak and strain
She recklessly throws herself under a train!

Vronsky is hopeless, completely bereft
In a whirlwind of torment from the life that she's left.
His only release is a longing for war,
To take up his headspace and shut fast the door;
By fighting for Russia is how he will cope,
Bravado and killing is his only hope.

Meanwhile, Levin is doubting his life -
He's mentally tortured with questions and strife
He gives up religion and quits Christianity
To find a more meaningful sense of morality.

He throws himself to hardest labour,
But will he absolve through devoted behaviour?
He's struggling within a crisis of meaning,
And finds not a hope or a thread of believing –

But lo! He meets this Theodore
Who gives him what he's looking for,
And he then tells the stupid berk
That he's already living for God through his work!

There's a massive storm and lightning bolts
And then in procrastination he halts,
Everyone's saved and his strong belief
Returns with a passion, oh what a relief!
He's totally awe-struck by what has occurred,
And he's learnt through the suffering that he's incurred,
He's finally found that great inner peace,
Freedom from chains and enormous release!

This voyage Tolstoy takes us through -
Can teach *us all* a thing or two:
Meaning in life, introspection to cope,
And learning, repentance, forgiveness, and hope;
But what is the message of Anna's affair
That Tolstoy is making which seems so unfair?

I guess what I'm thinking is through every season
The sinner discovers that love is their demon,
That heartbreak and pain does diminish their freedom
And love is the poison of truth and of reason!

Afterword

Thank you for purchasing Lyrical Literature; A whistle-stop tour of the classics – I hope you enjoyed reading it as much as I loved creating it!

I would be so grateful if you would consider leaving me a sparkling review on my Amazon page, which you can access directly by scanning this code.

Reviews help struggling authors like myself to reach more readers and enable me to publish more of my material, so do please leave one if you can!

Finally, thank you so much for your support! Your encouragement spurs me on to keep pursuing my dreams! Please keep Lyrical Literature in mind as a gift for those passionate about classic literature - sales depending, there may be another volume to come!

You can sign up to receive updates from Edwin Charles here
www.dyingtostayalive.com/blog

You can also follow Edwin Charles on Facebook
https://www.facebook.com/profile.php?id=100087761817249
Instagram
https://www.instagram.com/edwincharlesauthor/
TikTok
https://www.tiktok.com/@edwincharlesauthor

Acknowledgements

With huge thanks to my mother and Shirley Hook-Pattison (Antonia Abbott, author) for all their generous help with editing, and Patricia Moffett for the wonderful and imaginative cover design and illustrations.